T0357987

FIREWISE, FIRE-SAFE

How to Survive a Bushfire

Richard Whitaker

First published in Australia in 2004 by Reed New Holland
Published in 2020 by New Holland Publishers
Sydney • Auckland

Level 1, 178 Fox Valley Road, Wahroonga, NSW 2076, Australia
5/39 Woodside Ave, Northcote, Auckland 0627, New Zealand

newhollandpublishers.com

A record of this book is held at the National Library of Australia.

ISBN 9781760792428

Group Managing Director: Fiona Schultz
Publisher: Louise Egerton
Cover Designer: Yolanda La Gorcé
Designer: Andrew Davies
Production Director: Arlene Gippert
Printed in Australia by SOS Print + Media Group

10 9 8 7 6 5 4 3 2 1

Please note: Every effort has been made to ensure that the suggestions made
in this book are safe and appropriate. However, the author and publisher
accept no responsibility for any loss, injury or inconvenience sustained by
any person using this book.

Keep up with New Holland Publishers:
NewHollandPublishers
@newhollandpublishers

CONTENTS

EMERGENCY CONTACTS

Fire services are State-based organisations but they have broadly similar methods of operation. Fire warnings and total fire ban information can be obtained from the numbers listed. Of special note are the excellent, informative websites maintained by each fire service.

Detailed explanations of Bush Fire Alert levels can be found on page 38 – including Advice, Watch and Act, and Emergency Warning.

AUTHORITY	TELEPHONE CONTACTS	
Victorian Country Fire Authority	03 9262 8444	1800 226 226
New South Wales Rural Fire Service	02 8741 5555	1800 679 737
South Australia Country Fire Service	08 8115 3300	1800 362 361
Tasmania Fire Service	03 6173 2740	1800 000 699
Queensland Fire and Emergency Services	13 74 68	
Northern Territory Fire and Rescue Service	08 8999 3473	
Western Australia Fire and Emergency Services	13 3337	
ACT Rural Fire Service	02 6205 2927	

TO REPORT A BUSHFIRE, DIAL **000** IN ALL STATES.

During the fire season, fire danger levels and total fire ban information are also widely publicised in the media.

Please check the contact details for your local fire service regularly to make sure they are current.

Fire services are State-based organisations but they have broadly similar methods of operation. Fire warnings and total fire ban information can be obtained from the numbers listed. Of special note are the excellent, informative websites maintained by each fire service.

WEBSITE	FACEBOOK
www.cfa.vic.gov.au	CFA (Country Fire Authority)
www.rfs.nsw.gov.au	NSW Rural Fire Service
www.cfs.sa.gov.au	SA Country Fire Service
www.fire.tas.gov.au	Tasmania Fire Service
www.ruralfire.qld.gov.au	Queensland Fire and Emergency Services – QFES
www.pfes.nt.gov.au	Northern Territory Police, Fire and Emergency Services
www.dfes.wa.gov.au	Department of Fire and Emergency Services WA
esa.act.gov.au/rural-fire-service	ACT Rural Fire Service

INTRODUCTION

Bushfires are our most dangerous natural disaster, producing on average the highest number of deaths and injuries. No discussion of a bushfire can adequately capture the terrifying menace of a major blaze. The intense heat and thick, choking smoke cause fear, disorientation and panic among both people and animals in the path of the fire. Less well known is the frightening noise of a fire's approach. Survivors have described a terrifying roar, something like a jet aircraft taking off close by. People who have managed to escape a large fire are often deeply psychologically affected by the sheer terror they have experienced and may take some time to recover afterwards. The two main types of bushfire are forest fires and grass fires. Grass fires are normally not as intense as forest fires but can travel much faster, with speeds of around 25 kmph being recorded.

Although grass fires do not reach the same temperatures as forest fires, their speed makes them capable of causing widespread destruction and killing humans, livestock and wildlife caught in their path.

Bushfires often spread uncontrollably, depending on the type and nature of the available fuels, the surrounding terrain and the existing weather conditions, and represent a significant threat to the community. Bushfires can be ignited by natural phenomena such as lightning or spontaneous combustion but, tragically, are also often started by human activity such as smoking (discarded cigarette butts), the use of machinery (producing sparks) or arson.

THREE KILLERS

Bushfires pose three main threats to humans:

- radiant heat is the heat generated by the flames and can be deadly to both humans and animals.
- dehydration is caused by excessive sweating in the very hot conditions around a fire and can result in enervation and collapse.
- asphyxiation is caused by the inhalation of smoke or hot fumes and flames.

The information in this book will help you avoid the three killers through knowledge about fires and proper preparation.

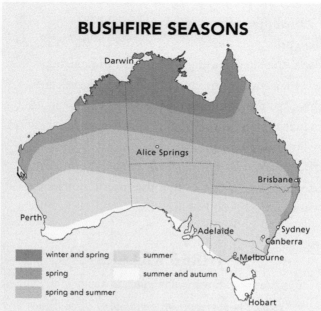

BUSHFIRE SEASONS

Maximum fire danger periods vary considerably with seasons across Australia and correspond with the occurrence of meteorological conditions most suitable for fires – low humidity, strong winds and high temperatures:

- NORTHERN AUSTRALIA – winter, which corresponds to the dry season across the tropical north
- SOUTHERN QUEENSLAND and NEW SOUTH WALES – spring and early summer
- VICTORIA AND TASMANIA – summer and autumn.

This north–south migration of peak fire danger periods is a consequence of seasonal weather patterns across Australia. However, these 'fire seasons' are only statistical averages – serious fires have occurred outside these periods. But in most cases this map is a good guide.

ONE

HOW BUSHFIRES BEHAVE

From watching television footage it often seems that bushfires are confusing, almost random phenomena. But, in fact they ignite and spread in quite a definite way and knowledge of this can improve your chances of survival.

How Bushfires Spread

Bushfires can spread in several different ways:

- surface fires feed off grass, leaf litter and low-lying shrubbery.
- crown fires travel at high speed along the top of the forest canopy.
- 'spot fires' begin when burning debris carried aloft falls to the ground downwind from the main fire, thereby starting new ones.
- underground fires travel along sub-surface root systems.

Severe bushfires include all four of the above and flame temperatures can reach over 1100°C, which is hot enough to melt copper. However, these temperatures are in the core of the fire; around the periphery, temperatures are normally much lower.

Bushfires tend to spread as a thin line of flame, with the thickness of the line roughly the same as the height. This means that the time a particular location on the ground is actually within the zone of flames is comparatively short, usually less than a minute. If a person trapped by the approach of a fire can find some type of protection for even this short period of time, they may survive (see also pages 52–3).

A fire that starts near the centre of a flat, grassy or forested field will spread in a roughly circular fashion if there is no wind. Its speed will depend upon the nature and 'dryness' of the fuel, as well as the temperature and humidity of the surrounding atmosphere.

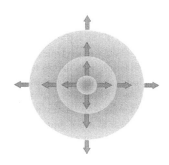

A. *No wind. Fire spreads in all different directions at equal speed to produce a circular burn pattern.*

However, wind creates a dramatically different pattern. Downwind, a fire front (F) moves much faster than the upwind section (U). The sides of the fire spread at a rate somewhere between the two. The burnt section is more elliptical in shape than the circular pattern shown in diagram A.

Near the ground, the smoke plume produced by the fire spreads out in the same direction as the low level winds, but as the smoke rises, it may change direction if the winds at higher levels also change direction.

B. *With wind. Fire spreads faster at F than at U, resulting in an elliptical burn pattern.*

Wind direction

How Fast Bushfires Travel

Severe bushfires typically move at about 15 kmph, with flames towering to 150 m. Grassfires can move as fast as 25 kmph, while non-severe forest fires normally travel at around 3 kmph, with flames up to 20 m high. Fires can appear to move much faster because of spot fires forming ahead of the main blaze. The speed at which a fire spreads depends on the amount and type of fuel, the weather conditions and the surrounding terrain.

HOW FUEL AFFECTS A BUSHFIRE

Vegetation and surface litter such as fallen leaves, branches and bark provide fuel for a fire to burn. The more of this there is, the higher the risk of a severe fire. Different types of fuel burn differently. The native eucalypt forests that cover much of south-eastern Australia are particularly flammable because of the oil in the leaves. Large areas of natural dry grass also burn fiercely under suitable conditions.

The pine trees grown commercially over parts of south-eastern Australia contain turpentine, which produces very different burning characteristics to the native vegetation. Plantation radiata pines have a very high fuel load and fire can move from treetop to treetop – in the form of 'crown fires' – much faster than in a eucalypt forest.

Obviously the 'dryness' of the fuel will also be a major factor. Damp fuel is difficult to ignite, but dry fuel, often the result of extended dry periods, ignites easily and promotes rapid spread.

THE EFFECT OF WEATHER ON BUSHFIRES

Humidity. The moisture content of the air, is measured by an instrument called a hygrometer. Low humidity means the fire spreads faster.

Temperature. Contrary to popular belief, it is not necessary to have high temperatures to support a bushfire. Some quite severe fires have occurred in comparatively mild temperatures. However, high temperatures certainly raise the potential for severe blazes. This is mainly because hot conditions assist in further drying out available fuel, and also assist in the initiation of 'spot fires'.

Wind. The greater the wind speed, the faster the spread of the fire. Wind feeds oxygen to the fire, assists flames in reaching into adjacent vegetation and enhances fire 'spotting'. It has been estimated that given set temperature and humidity conditions, doubling the wind speed will quadruple the rate of spread of the fire.

Wind is measured by an instrument called an anenometer, usually in kilometres per hour or knots (1 knot = 1.85 kmph); knots are usually used to describe the wind over the ocean.

HOW THE TERRAIN AFFECTS A BUSHFIRE

Fire tends to accelerate up slopes because the flames can reach under the canopy of the trees further uphill, increasing the chance of treetop ignition. Conversely, the rate of spread downhill tends to be somewhat reduced because of lesser exposure of the canopy to the flames. Fire is one of the few phenomena in nature that travels faster uphill than on the flat. For every 10 degree increase in slope the speed of the fire roughly doubles.

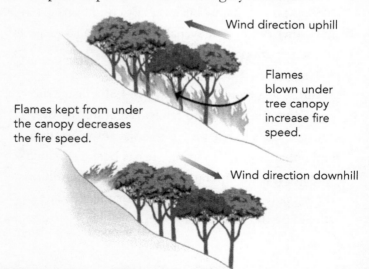

Wind direction uphill

Flames blown under tree canopy increase fire speed.

Flames kept from under the canopy decreases the fire speed.

Wind direction downhill

THE EFFECT OF DROUGHT ON BUSHFIRES

Drought is normally part of the lead-up to a severe fire season. But there have been exceptions to this rule. Every fire season is different and produces its own unique set of conditions.

The extent and dryness of fuel directly affects the nature of fires. Over tropical Australia, the winter dry season virtually guarantees that the fuel will be dry and suitable for burning. However, the type of vegetation in the area is usually not as thick or as flammable as the vast eucalypt forests of southern Australia, and fires across the top end are not normally as intense.

Drought is often the precursor of a bad fire season in the southern States; it creates tinder dry, easily ignited vegetation. The devastating Ash Wednesday bushfires of 1983 and the Canberra fire disaster of 2003 were both preceded by acute drought that affected much of eastern Australia during 1982 and 2002 respectively. The calamitous 'Black Friday' bushfires of January 1939 followed a record dry season across parts of southern Victoria, which recorded its driest July-to-December rainfall to date.

However, there are exceptions to this rule. One notorious example was the immensely destructive

Tasmanian fires of February 1967. During early spring of 1966, bountiful rain fell across much of Tasmania. As the warmer weather arrived, vegetation grew vigorously, resulting in a thick cover of grass and undergrowth, particularly around Hobart. But during November, the wet weather pattern abruptly ceased, and the heavy vegetation build-up of the previous two months rapidly dried out and became highly flammable. Although this was only a short dry period compared with the prolonged droughts of 1982 and 2002, it was enough to form the first link in the chain that led to the February conflagration across much of southern Tasmania.

In more recent times the disastrous 'Black Saturday' conflagration that swept across Victoria on 7th February 2009 was preceded by good rains across much of the state in December 2008, followed by very dry weather in January 2009.

In late 2019 widespread bushfires erupted across eastern Australia, preceded by record or near record dry conditions and high temperatures from June to December.

Other effects of drought include the following:

- Dried-out logs and tree stumps continue to burn after the main blaze has passed through.
- Dry undergrowth and forest canopy tend to

'flare', causing crown fires that travel quickly through treetops.

- Drought prior to the fire season can make it too dangerous to conduct hazard-reduction burns, resulting in a heavier load of fuel.
- 'Dry' thunderstorms that occur during drought years generate lightning that can start fires, but little, if any, rain to put them out.
- Drought is normally associated with a higher than average number of clear nights and, during winter, more frequent frosts. This dries grasslands and increases their flammability coming into the fire season.
- Dams and creeks either dry up or retain little water. This significantly reduces the water supply available to firefighters, both on the ground and for aerial bombardment.
- Existing firebreaks are normally less efficient during drought years. In very dry weather, embers travelling ahead of the fire can easily jump quite wide firebreaks and cause ignition on the other side.
- Drought-affected trees are usually highly stressed and tend to drop more leaves than normal, producing more dry leaf litter on the forest floor.
- Drought often results in water restrictions that prevent householders from keeping their gardens green, resulting in dry, flammable surroundings.

The Worst Possible Scenario

Extreme fire weather occurs when there is simultaneously plentiful dry fuel, strong winds, low humidity and high temperature. Under these conditions, fire spreads rapidly and is generally difficult, if not impossible, to control. Weather patterns that produce such conditions have definite characteristics well known to meteorologists and vary throughout Australia.

SOUTH-EASTERN AUSTRALIA

A dangerous fire situation that sometimes occurs over South Australia, Victoria and Tasmania is often associated with the approach of a cold front during summer. This can produce a burst of hot, dry northerly winds running ahead of the front, ideal for the rapid spread of fires.

NEW SOUTH WALES AND SOUTHERN QUEENSLAND

In these areas, spring and early summer tend to be the peak fire danger periods. One of the most potentially dangerous situations occurs when an intense low-pressure cell develops near Tasmania. This generates strong westerly winds along the east coast of the mainland and can produce very low humidity and high temperatures.

WESTERN AUSTRALIA

In southern parts of Western Australia, summer winds from the east to north-east originating in the inland tend to be very dry and hot. Such winds can be caused by a strong high-pressure cell developing over South Australia and can occasionally lead to extreme fire danger.

TROPICAL AUSTRALIA

Over the tropical north, winter is very dry, and high pressure cells located over New South Wales or South Australia can direct dry southeasterly winds over northern Australia. Although the resulting temperatures are not as high as in the summer northerlies over the south-eastern States, conditions are still conducive to bushfires.

INSURANCE PAYOUT

Bushfires have the potential to cost the insurance industry many millions of dollars. But, this dollar count is relatively small in comparison to floods, severe thunderstorms and tropical cyclones, which together account for nearly 90% of insurance costs.

CHANGES AND THE DEAD MAN'S ZONE

The Dead Man's Zone is the area of a fire in most danger from a change of wind. Those battling a blaze need to have a pre-planned escape route in case the fire suddenly surges towards them due to a wind change. Firefighters should never enter an area unless there's a way of getting out quickly.

Wind from the north

Fast-moving and dangerous fire front

Some cold fronts produce no rain or thunderstorms. However, the associated change in wind direction, from the northerlies ahead of the front to westerlies or south westerlies following the change, can magnify the size and danger of a fire front. In such cases, the fall in temperature after the front does not significantly reduce the rate of fire spread. Sudden wind changes, particularly associated with

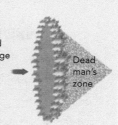

Fast-moving and dangerous fire front

Wind change from the west

Dead man's zone

dry cold fronts, can certainly produce dangerous firefighting situations, and have been responsible for several tragedies. This has led to the concept of the so-called 'Dead Man's Zone' amongst firefighters.

TWO

PREPARING FOR THE BUSHFIRE SEASON

Thorough preparation before the bushfire season can greatly increase your chances of surviving and perhaps saving your home and property.

Preparing Your Home and Property

❏ Make a 'green oasis' around your home
(see page 24).

❏ Learn how to prevent burning embers entering
your home (see page 25).

❏ Keep a ladder inside for access to the roof
cavity in case fires start there, and another that
will be easily accessible from the garden to reach
the exterior of the roof.

❏ Practise blocking your down pipes – with tennis
balls (for round pipes) or rags (for square pipes)
– and filling the gutters with water. Rehearse this
procedure so you know that a certain method
will work. Don't leave it until a bushfire is
approaching to begin experimentation.

❏ Make sure you have appropriate firefighting
equipment and maintain it in good working
order (see page 33).

❏ Ensure that hoses fitted to outside taps can
reach all parts of your home. Keep sprinkler
attachments handy.

❏ If you have a swimming pool, purchase a pump
to pump water from the pool onto the blaze
(see page 34).

❏ Store all flammable items, such as petrol, gas
bottles, paint and firewood, well away from your
home.

❏ Have a battery-powered radio in working order
   and with spare batteries, together with a supply
   of candles for emergency lighting.

Clearing firebreaks

Firebreaks are simply areas where fires won't burn
or will burn only slowly. They can be natural features
such as streams or elongated rocky areas or other
areas where vegetation is sparse.

Large-scale firebreaks are often cleared in the bush
to allow access for firefighting vehicles, but you
can construct them on a smaller scale around the
buildings on your property.

To construct your own firebreak, use a rake or shovel
to clear grass and leaf litter for at least 20 m around
your home, shed, garage or barn. You can also
remove vegetation by poisoning, burning (see pages
30–31), grading, rotary hoeing or a combination of
these. Whilst this may be labour intensive the first
time around, once established, the firebreak will be
easier to maintain.

Clear the area at least once a week during the fire
season and after a period of strong winds when litter
has built up.

MAKE A 'GREEN OASIS' AROUND YOUR HOME

Research has shown that a well-maintained and 'green' garden around your home significantly reduces the chance of it catching fire.

- ❏ Keep all vegetation, leaf litter and tree branches well away from your home and clear firebreaks around buildings (see page 23).
- ❏ Remove dead branches from nearby trees and shrubs.
- ❏ Keep the grass short during the fire season.
- ❏ Clear gutters of leaves and debris.
- ❏ Close all exterior gaps under the roof or that allow access under your home.
- ❏ Fit wire screens to doors and windows.
- ❏ Keep all shrubs near your home well pruned.
- ❏ Keep the surroundings, including the lawn, watered and green. During drought, use tank water or water pumped up from a bore or nearby dam, or collect water from the washing up, washing machines, baths and showers in buckets and use it to water the garden and lawn.

PROTECT YOUR HOME FROM BURNING EMBERS

Burning leaves and embers can blow into nooks and crannies, the space between the roof and ceiling, under the house and into the gutters and ignite a fire. To prevent this:

- ❏ Fit wire screens to doors, windows and ventilators.
- ❏ Close all gaps under the house and under roof eaves.
- ❏ Cover the top of any chimneys with wire mesh.
- ❏ Fit metal screens across your fireplace.
- ❏ Install sprinklers along the line of the roof eaves (see page 77).

(See also chapter 9, Designing a Fire-resistant Home.)

Preparing Yourself

❑ Keep emergency services contact details (see page 4) in a prominent place.

❑ Check your fire insurance status. Fire victims have sometimes discovered too late that they are either uninsured or inadequately insured.

❑ Assemble a suitable set of clothes for firefighting (see page 43). Include a blanket that you can wet before throwing it over yourself as protection during the fire.

❑ Consider taking a first-aid course (see also chapter 6, First Aid).

❑ Keep a well-equipped first-aid kit in your home (see page 28).

❑ Consider joining your local bush fire brigade (see page 29).

❑ Have a basic knowledge of fire behaviour (see chapter 1, How Fires Behave).

❑ Think about whether you would stay and fight a fire or whether you would evacuate (see page 40). Remember that, depending on what State you live in, you may be ordered to leave by the police during an emergency.

❑ Be prepared to evacuate should the situation become untenable. Make an evacuation plan. Formulate an alternative plan in case your first route is cut.

❏ Make a list, in priority order, of what to pack in your car should you have to evacuate (see page 44). Keep important family documents in one folder that you can quickly grab. Include household insurance papers in case of a dispute after the fire.

❏ Keep a mobile phone in service – phone lines are sometimes downed during a fire.

MOBILE PHONES AND FIRES

Mobile phones have become the backbone of modern domestic communication so its important to keep your phone fully charged during the run up to a fire. If general power outages develop you may not be able to recharge your battery.

Also remember that in a fire situation the network may be disabled. This can result from fires directly damaging communication towers and in such a situation it could mean no texting, calls, internet browsing or social media. These are all valuable tools to use but they are vulnerable in a severe fire situation.

FIRST-AID KIT

Remember it's not only burns people may suffer in a bushfire environment – cuts and bruises, spider and insect bites, foreign matter in the eyes and ankle sprains are also common.

Your medical kit should include:

- ❏ *First Aid Quick Reference* (St John Ambulance)
- ❏ non-adherent dressings (for small injuries)
- ❏ wound dressings in sizes 13, 14 and 15 (for larger wounds)
- ❏ cold compresses
- ❏ saline solution
- ❏ triangular bandages
- ❏ roll bandages
- ❏ gauze squares
- ❏ scissors, tweezers and latex gloves
- ❏ alcohol wipes
- ❏ sterile eye pads
- ❏ Stingose™ gel
- ❏ tape
- ❏ disposable towels (e.g. Chux™)
- ❏ non-stick burns sheet.

Inspect the kit regularly and replace any products that have reached their 'use-by' date.

Good quality first-aid kits can be purchased from chemists, many department and hardware stores, as well as from some motorists organisations.

JOIN YOUR LOCAL
BUSH FIRE BRIGADE

If you live in or near the bush, think about joining the local bush fire brigade. These volunteers are dedicated to patrolling their local area and protecting citizens from bushfires. They are trained in firefighting and maintaining the emergency vehicles associated with their tasks.

Brigades may sometimes be deployed far from their local area, even interstate in some cases, where large fires have overwhelmed the capacity of local firefighters.

Local brigades are a great source of knowledge about bushfires, particularly with reference to the local area. They play a valuable role in community education in all aspects of fire safety and fire prevention.

A good example is the New South Wales Rural Fire Service – the largest volunteer fire service in the world with nearly 72,500 members that are organised into 2002 local brigades. In addition to the volunteers, this massive organisation employs a large staff at head office as well as at regional offices and fire control centres.

The RFS is headed by a commissioner who reports directly to the New South Wales Minister for Emergency Services, and who has the responsibility to coordinate and direct the efforts of his firefighting forces during major fire outbreaks.

For further information contact your State organization (see page 4).

BURNING OFF

Land-holders can reduce the fuel load on their properties in anticipation of the coming fire season by 'burning off' or, more technically, conducting a hazard-reduction burn. This can also include the construction of firebreaks (see page 23). However, before undertaking any such activity, follow the correct procedures for your State.

DURING THE FIRE SEASON

During the official fire season (called the Bushfire Danger Period) for a particular area, you will usually need a Fire Permit before lighting any fire. Check with your State bushfire service for details (see phone numbers on page 4).

A Fire Permit authorises the nominated person to light a fire on the land specified for the purpose outlined in the permit. However, a permit can be revoked if the weather conditions change, causing an increase in fire danger.

OUTSIDE THE FIRE SEASON

Outside the fire season, it may not be necessary to obtain a formal permit before conducting a hazard reduction burn, but check with your local fire service before you begin. You may still need to notify neighbouring landowners and local fire authorities.

Have firefighting equipment on hand and helpers available to ensure that any fire you light cannot escape beyond the bounds of your property.

LIGHTING FIRES WITHOUT AUTHORITY

Because of the massive threat that bushfires pose to life and property, you can be severely penalized if you are careless with fire.

Burning off without a permit or allowing a fire to escape onto another property or crown land can attract substantial fines. If fires started under these circumstances cause death, injury or property damage, heavy fines or even a jail sentence can result.

Similar penalties can be imposed if you start a serious fire through carelessness or neglect, such as a discarded cigarette or improperly operated machinery during periods of high fire danger.

Preparing For Your livestock

Follow these guidelines to prevent, or at least minimise, the loss of farm animals during a fire:

❏ prepare a cleared paddock nearby or an area of irrigated pasture to where stock can escape or be moved should a fire overrun the property.

❏ keep stockyards or holding paddocks as clean and clear as possible, with shade and drinking areas available.

❏ maintain a cleared area at least 20 m wide around reserves of fodder, such as hay stacks, hay sheds and silos, which may be the only food left for your animals after a fire has passed through. Slash, plough, or use herbicides to clear around them. If using the latter, keep poisons away from feed.

Fencing

Bushfires will often damage fencing, particularly the traditional type that consists of wooden posts mounted with strands of wire. To minimise damage, use herbicides to keep the zone along the fence line clear of fuel. Make sure that this will not poison livestock.

If erecting new fences, use fire-resistant materials, such as concrete posts instead of wood.

FIREFIGHTING EQUIPMENT

HOSES Check them regularly for leaks or 'kinks' and repair or replace if necessary. Keep them attached to the taps. Use brass fittings as they will not melt in the heat as plastic fittings may do.

RAKES AND SHOVELS are useful for clearing away burning debris near your home and for clearing firebreaks (see page 23). You can also use a shovel to throw earth on small spot fires. Make sure the handles are not broken or split and are firmly attached to the heads. Store them in a place where they are readily accessible.

LADDERS To allow quick access to the roof, store ladders in a handy location under cover. Check them regularly for signs of deterioration. Develop a safety routine to prevent falls from roofs and ladders: establish firm ladder resting points and identify easy access areas to the roof.

BUCKETS OR WATER CONTAINERS Make sure they have no holes and the handles are functional. Know where they are so you can rapidly fill and deploy.

THE 'McLEOD TOOL' is a rake specially designed for firefighting. It has a metal head, one side of which is serrated to function as a normal rake. The other edge is sharpened and can be used for cutting, chipping and scraping.

FIRE BEATERS You can make these simple tools yourself. Just nail or wire a strip of canvas, blanket or rubber about half a metre long to the end of a broom handle. They can be used to extinguish small spot fires. Fire beaters are also available commercially.

PUMPS Many homes have been saved by the owners pumping water from a pool or dam onto the approaching fire. A petrol- or diesel-powered pump is best, as electricity lines are often down during a bushfire.

SPRINKLER SYSTEMS Your garden sprinklers, as well as specially installed firefighting sprinkler systems (see page 77), provide good all-round protection for your home.

KNAPSACK SPRAYS Although quite old fashioned, this fire-fighting appliance is still regarded as an important piece of equipment and is useful in controlling small spot fires around a domestic property. A polythene water tank carried in a harness on the person's back is connected to a spray nozzle device. Water is usually sprayed by pumping a handle. The tank contains around 15 L of water.

They are useful for extinguishing small fires before they become more serious or for wetting down key areas around your home when a fire is approaching, but are not suitable for large blazes. You can buy knapsack sprays at large hardware stores.

USING A CHAINSAW

It's useful to have a chainsaw on hand when a bushfire threatens. Use it to quickly prepare firebreaks, remove overhanging branches from around your home and clear fallen trees.

However, in inexperienced hands a chainsaw is a highly dangerous machine. If you plan to buy or hire one, take a course on how to maintain and operate it. Chainsaw training courses are available from a variety of sources, including TAFE colleges, agricultural organisations and bushfire groups. The training offered by bushfire authorities normally includes:

- cross cutting
- simple tree felling
- problem tree felling
- general safety and maintenance tips.

FIRE DANGER RATINGS

These display the level of fire danger: Low/Moderate, High, Very high, Severe, extreme or catastrophic. (In Victoria 'catastrophic' is replaced with 'Code Red') These ratings are calculated from predicted levels of temperature, wind speed, relative humidity and fuel state. They describe how readily a fire will develop and its subsequent speed of movement.

Fire danger ratings for both forests and grasslands are prepared daily by the Bureau of Meteorology during the fire season. In areas that include both types of country the higher danger rating will apply. Roadside fire danger meters are usually metal signs mounted on a stand at a conspicuous location that is readily visible to passing drivers. Usually they display a semicircle with standard colours for the

different danger levels as shown in the diagram. Occasionally a rectangular sign, which displays the same information on an elongated rectangle divided into the six fire danger ratings, is used.

During the fire season the indicator on the sign is set on the calculated fire danger rating. This may be done by manually setting the device or using electronic methods. In the latter case the hand can be illuminated so that the sign can be seen at night.

TOTAL FIRE BAN

A State bushfire authority will impose a total fire ban over a particular area when it believes that the fire danger is too high to safely light a fire in the open. Total fire bans imply slightly different things in different States but, in general, when a total fire ban is in force it is illegal to light any form of fire in the open. There are exceptions, including properly sited gas barbecues, but always check local regulations before assuming any such exception.

If the predicted fire danger for the next day is Catastrophic (or Code Red in Victoria) fire authorities will usually declare a total fire ban for that day, which normally covers the 24-hour period from midnight to midnight. Depending on the situation fire authorities may also declare a total fire ban for fire danger ratings less than Catastrophic – such as Severe or Extreme.

During the months of the fire season, the Bureau of Meteorology forecasts the fire danger for the following day, using predicted temperatures, relative humidity and wind speeds. These fire danger ratings are distributed to the public through the media, the internet and mobile phones. The ratings are also displayed to thousands of passing motorists on daily updated roadside fire meters (see page 36).

Once fires are burning Emergency Warning Levels are issued that enable you to gauge the seriousness of your situation:

ADVICE: The fire has started. No immediate danger but monitor the situation.

WATCH AND ACT: The threat is increasing. You will need to start taking action to protect your household.

EMERGENCY WARNING: The highest alert level. You may be in danger and you need to take immediate action – likely evacuate.

THREE

WHEN THE FIRE APPROACHES

When a fire is approaching, the first thing you need to do is decide whether you will evacuate or stay and fight the fire.

Fight or Flight?

There is no definitive answer to the basic question: fight or flight? Every situation is different, with factors such as local vegetation, exposure to wind, intensity of the approaching blaze, your level of preparation, and availability of firefighting equipment all being relevant.

Make sure you are well informed before making your decision whether to evacuate or stay and fight the fire. Be prepared to re-evaluate in the face of changing circumstances.

There is no doubt that many homes have been saved by residents who stayed to fight, just as there is no doubt that many lives have been saved by evacuation. But research has shown that if you do stay to fight the fire, there is an increased chance that your home will survive. When a severe fire is approaching, police or firefighting authorities may recommend (or require) residents to evacuate (see page 68).

Consider evacuation if:

- you are not confident that your home can be defended because of its position or construction or lack of preparation.
- there are children, elderly or disabled people in your household who may have difficulty in

handling the situation or who may not be able to flee rapidly if things deteriorate.
- the fire becomes overwhelming and you are aware of a safe refuge that you can reach.

If, on the other hand, you decide to stay and fight, it is absolutely essential that you are well prepared (see Chapter 2, Preparing for the Bushfire Season).

EVACUATION GOLDEN RULES

- If the predicted fire danger is Catastrophic (or Code Red in Victoria) evacuation is always the best policy.
- Do it early.
- Know your destination.
- If in a car, drive safely: slow down if visibility is poor due to thick smoke; watch out for wildlife or domestic animals that may veer onto the road as they flee the fire; make way for emergency vehicles; beware of debris, including tree branches, falling onto the road and try to drive around, rather than over, the top.

In the Home

❏ Phone 000 and report the fire. Don't assume the fire authorities know about it.

❏ Listen to the radio and/or watch local and State news for fire information.

❏ Keep children, elderly people and pets inside the home. Make sure they have plenty to drink and monitor their movements carefully. It's important that everyone stays together.

❏ Turn off the gas supply.

❏ Close all windows and doors and block any gaps from the inside with wet towels to prevent entry of burning embers. You can also seal around windows and doors with duct tape.

❏ Fill the bath, basins, kitchen sink, buckets and large saucepans with water as an emergency supply and to extinguish any small internal blazes.

❏ Remove curtains and move furniture away from windows. Fire can burst through windows and ignite items nearby.

❏ Dress protectively (see What To Wear on page 43).

❏ Pack important belongings ready to load into the car in case of evacuation (see What To Pack on page 44).

❏ Charge your mobile phone.

WHAT TO WEAR

Before going outside, dress protectively. Shorts, t-shirts and thongs do not provide adequate protection against heat or flying embers.

DO WEAR:

- wool, denim and cotton clothing
- loose-fitting long pants and a long-sleeved shirt, or a pair of sturdy overalls
- cotton or woollen socks and a sturdy pair of leather boots or shoes
- woollen or canvas gloves
- goggles to protect your eyes from thick smoke
- a wide-brimmed or 'hard' hat
- a scarf or large handkerchief you can tie around your neck and draw over your nose and mouth to protect you from smoke inhalation. For maximum protection, keep it damp.

NOTE It is a good idea to leave your ears uncovered as they are particularly heat sensitive and can warn you of a rapid increase in temperature.

DO NOT WEAR synthetics such as nylon or rayon. These can be flammable and will stick to your skin in conditions of extreme heat.

WHAT TO PACK

- Important documents such as household insurance papers, passports, birth and marriage certificates.
- Wallet containing credit cards, money and driver's licence.
- Mobile phone.
- Photo albums.
- Valuables such as jewellery and paintings.
- If room and time permits, a change of clothing for each family member.
- Children's toys and pets' equipment.

Outside the Home

❏ Close window shutters if you have them.

❏ Replace any external wire flyscreens that have been temporarily removed as they can prevent small embers from lodging on window sills.

❏ Plug down pipes and fill the gutters with water.

❏ Bring all doormats inside. These can catch alight if exposed to hot embers and result in a fire developing literally on your front doorstep.

❏ Move all potentially combustible material well away from the house.

❏ Fill your knapsack spray (if you have one) with water ready for use.

❏ Ensure that all hoses and sprinkler systems are connected.

❏ Place your garden sprinklers on the side of
   the property facing the fire and turn them on.
   Although the mains pressure may fall and the
   hoses may eventually melt, wetting down the
   garden with the garden sprinklers can help your
   firefighting sprinkler system (see page 77) to
   save your home. Keep all sprinklers going until
   the fire is well past.

❏ Hose down all shrubbery, the roof, and house
   walls on the side of the approaching fire and
   douse any small fires that have already begun.
   Remember that the water pressure may have
   dropped well below its normal level around this
   time because of heavy usage in the area.

❏ If you intend pumping water from a pool or
   dam, make sure that your pump is fully fuelled
   and ready for action.

In the Bush on Foot

❏ Observe carefully from which direction and at
   what speed the fire is approaching. The low-
   level smoke will give you some idea of this –
   if smoke is increasing, the fire may be heading
   towards you. Try to move away from the
   smoke to avoid smoke inhalation and maximise
   visibility.

❑ Don't try and run directly away from the fire
if it's moving fast. Instead, move to the left
or right of the fire; in most cases choose the
downhill side (unless the bush is too thick).
This is because fires tend to move more slowly
downhill (and more quickly uphill!) in a given set
of wind and vegetation conditions (see page 51).

❑ Look for a place of refuge. A dam, creek or
river is ideal, and even a wooden building can
provide shelter from the heat of the flames for
a short period until the main fire has passed.
If in a camping area, a public building such as a
brick toilet block can provide good protection.
DO NOT jump into a raised water tank as the
water can boil in the extreme heat of the fire
(see page 70).

❑ Move towards an area of lesser vegetation, such
as a forest clearing or paddock. Less fuel means
reduced fire intensity.

❑ If you are in a family or group try and stay
together. Individuals wandering off in different
directions can greatly complicate the situation.

In Your Car

❏ Park the car in a clear area with the keys in the ignition ready for a quick getaway.

❏ Close all doors, windows and vents to keep out smoke.

❏ Pack some woollen blankets with which to cover yourself against the fire. Ideally these should be wet, but even dry blankets will provide some protection.

❏ Store some bottles of drinking water in the car.

❏ Keep a map of the local area in the car so that you'll always know where you are. Your escape from the area will depend on where and how the fire is approaching and whether you head in the right direction.

❏ Drive with your hazard lights and headlights on to help keep you visible to other traffic and pedestrians in thick bushfire smoke.

❏ Drive slowly and carefully; you don't want to escape the fire only to end up in a car crash caused by speeding in low-visibility conditions.

FOUR

WHEN THE FIRE ARRIVES

The worst place to be in a bushfire is outdoors. You are safer in a car than outside, and safer again in a house than in a car. But even if you are caught outside there is a good chance of survival if you take certain precautions.

In the Home

Homes do not normally burn down in the first
10 minutes as the flames are actually moving
through. Instead, they tend to be ignited by embers,
radiant heat from the fire or by materials near the
house catching on fire, and they normally take more
than an hour to burn down. This means that if you
shelter inside the house from the flames as they
pass across and then emerge to extinguish any spot
fires, there is a good chance you will survive the
blaze. However in very high intensity fires houses
can ignite and burn on a much faster time scale.
The 2009 Victorian bushfires were a tragic example.
Evacuation is the only option in fires like these.

❏ If you are not evacuating, go inside your home
and stay away from windows. These may shatter
as the flames reach the house.

❏ Dress yourself and all of your family protectively
(see page 43).

❏ Drink plenty of water, preferably every ten
minutes, as the hot, dry air around bushfires can
cause dehydration. Do not drink alcohol – it will
dehydrate you even more.

❏ If your home is on fire and you can't extinguish it,
leave and move to burnt ground away from the fire.
Remain in the area if it's safe to do so; don't hike
into the bush where it may be difficult to find you.

❏ If you have a manhole in the ceiling, check inside the roof cavity and extinguish any fires that may have started there.

Outside the Home

- After the main fire has passed, check your home and yard and extinguish any spot fires with whatever equipment you have.
- Check your livestock and move them to safety if necessary.

USING A FIRE BEATER

Wet your fire beater (see page 34) and use it to beat out any small spot fires, either ahead of the main blaze or after the fire front has passed. Keep the fabric moist by periodically dipping it in water. You can also cover your nose and mouth with wet fabric to reduce smoke inhalation.

In the Bush on Foot

If you are caught on foot in the open with a fire bearing down, don't panic: many people have survived this situation by using the following guidelines:

❏ Cover your skin as much as possible with your clothing. If you have a towel, blanket or hessian bag, use these too.

❏ In general, don't try to outrun the fire or travel uphill – remember that, depending on the vegetation, fire tends to accelerate uphill and lose speed downhill (see page 14). Burnt ground can provide some safety. Also, don't try to run through flames unless you can see a clear area immediately on the other side.

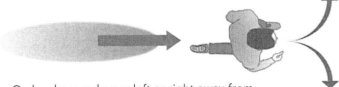

On level ground, veer left or right away from the direction of the fire's approach

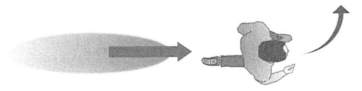

On sloping ground, usually veer towards the low side away from the direction of the fire's approach

A blanket provides protection from flames and radiant heat.

❑ Hold a wet towel or handkerchief across your nose and mouth to minimise the amount of smoke you inhale and protect your lungs.

❑ Get down low where there may be less smoke – smoke and hot gases tend to rise.

❑ If it becomes apparent that the flames are about to sweep across you, lie face down on the ground, if possible under an overhang, or in a hollow under a rock, large log or downed tree for protection from the heat of the flames.

A hollow will also provide some protection against smoke inhalation. Leave this position after the fire has passed over you as it may catch fire around this time. You can also jump into a dam or river, but not a water tank (see page 70).

❏ If you are able to cover yourself in a damp woollen blanket, together with loose soil (see page 74), this will give you some protection against the radiant heat of a fire passing over. People have survived high-intensity fires in this way.

Jump into a dam or river, stay low, and cover your mouth and nose with a wet cloth.

In the Car

Try not to drive near bushfires in the first place, but if you find yourself confronted with a bushfire, follow these recommendations:

❏ Don't try to drive through flames or thick smoke. The flames might be running parallel with the road, and trying to drive through might expose the car to a prolonged period of fire and high radiant heat.

❏ If you can't go any further, try to stop in an area of minimum vegetation rather than on a road in heavily timbered country. Pull over, leaving the engine running to power the air conditioner (on recycled air – air from outside will be smoky). Switch on your hazard lights and headlights so that you are more likely to be seen from another vehicle.

❏ Close the windows (and vents if you have no air conditioner) and lie down below window level as the flames pass across. Cover yourself with a blanket or rug to protect yourself from the radiant heat.

❏ As the flames reach the car, stay inside; don't attempt to flee the vehicle. It is most unlikely that the fuel tank will explode in the comparatively short time the fire takes to pass across your area. Of far greater danger is the radiant heat from the flames, and the car will give you some protection from this.

❑ Assess the situation after the flames have passed across. If the car is on fire, exit the vehicle and move away from the fire to already burnt ground.

FIVE

AFTER THE FIRE

Strangely, the period immediately following the fire can be almost as dangerous as the fire itself. Buildings still standing may be unsafe, trees may be still smouldering or have fallen across roads or structures, and electricity wires may be down. Survivors of fire have been injured or killed by these types of hazards.

Cleaning Up

❏ Dress for safety in the same clothing as for fighting the fire. Use thick gloves and a hat. Wear a long-sleeved shirt and long trousers to avoid scratches and sunburn. Boots or sturdy shoes are a must to protect feet from smouldering embers and branches, and nails exposed in burned timber. In rural settings, if wooden fence posts have been burned, lengths of barbed wire may be lying on the ground, creating hazards for humans and stock.

❏ Promptly clean and disinfect cuts and scratches.

❏ Drink plenty of water to avoid dehydration – conditions following the fire may still be hot and dry.

❏ Do not re-enter your home if it has been partly destroyed. The structure may be unstable. Opening a door or pulling aside some debris on the floor may trigger a catastrophic collapse which could kill or injure.

❏ Do not attempt to clear fallen branches or tree trunks from the roof or those leaning against the house. Live powerlines may be down or hanging about in an unstable fashion creating the potential for electric shock. Tree limbs may be smouldering, With the bark covering a bed of red hot coals. Trees and branches dropped onto already weakened roofs by inexperienced householders can cause further damage and expose the interior to rain. Leave this work to emergency services.

❑ Do not work with chainsaws unless you are trained and experienced (see page 35). Leave this work to the professionals.

❑ Be careful when clearing burnt branches or logs from around your property. These can continue smouldering for several days after the fire and cause burns if handled or stepped upon (see page 74–5 for more information.)

❑ Do not attempt to reconnect gas, electricity and water yourself. Contact the relevant authority.

❑ Discard all food, drink and medicines exposed to the fire. Discard food in refrigerators and freezers after three hours or so without power. When power is re-established do not refreeze thawed items as this is a health risk.

Secure Your Property

It is a sad fact that looting occasionally follows in the path of a fire, when many residents have left the area. Secure your property as best you can following these guidelines:

❏ Notify the local police if you will be leaving your home.

❏ Board over windows and doors if you don't intend to stay in your home.

❏ Cover damaged roofs and walls with tarpaulins to prevent further damage from rain.

❏ Remove money and valuables, identification papers, cash, credit cards, driver's licence, banking and financial documents and insurance policies.

❏ Take with you medicines that were not exposed to fire or water, and personal aids such as eyeglasses, dentures, prosthetic devices and hearing aids.

❏ If you are renting the property, be sure to contact the landlord or managing real estate agent as soon as possible if you intend vacating.

Emergency Accommodation and Assistance

You may be in need of temporary accommodation. Check with your insurance company to see if you are covered for this or perhaps entitled to a cash advance on your final settlement. If you are not insured or there is no immediate solution, contact the Department of Community Services or the Salvation Army. They may be able to provide you with short term relief while you assess your situation. In the past, bushfire relief funds built on donations from the public have also assisted the uninsured.

Send details of your new location to:

❏ friends, family and neighbours

❏ your insurance company

❏ your employer

❏ your children's school

❏ post office and delivery services

❏ gas, water and electricity suppliers.

Dealing with Trauma

After a bushfire life does not always immediately return to normal. People are often deeply shocked by the experience and traumatised by the loss of loved ones, pets or homes. Even well after the event they may suffer from anxiety, insomnia and depression. If you think you are suffering from any of these conditions, consult your local doctor for advice or a referral for specialist treatment. Telephone hotlines are sometimes established to assist traumatised survivors, and organisations such as Lifeline which offer telephone counselling services may also be helpful.

INSURANCE

- If you are insured, contact the insurance company immediately.
- Compile a list of items destroyed or damaged by fire, the more detail the better, even down to the number of CDs lost and quantity of food ruined.
- Keep receipts for all money spent on repairs or replacement of household items. You may need these for your insurance claim.
- Store damaged items in a separate area where the insurance assessor can inspect them.

SIX

FIRST AID

Evaluate the seriousness of the injury and call an ambulance (000) if necessary. Following are some basic treatments for injuries that may result from bushfires.

In a bushfire environment, as well as shock, burns and smoke inhalation, a variety of other injuries can occur, often associated with unstable structures, falling trees, barbed wire on the ground and nails protruding from timber. In all cases, evaluate the seriousness of the injury and call an ambulance (000) if necessary. Below are some basic treatments for injuries that may result from bushfires. You can perform these treatments whilst waiting for the ambulance. When caring for others, make sure that you maintain your own and their safety.

BURNS

- If the person is alight, have them STOP, DROP AND ROLL on the ground. Smother flames with thick clothing such as a coat, or a blanket.
- Pour cold water (low-pressure) over the burn, continuing for about 20 minutes.
- Remove smouldering clothing but don't pull clothing across a burnt face.
- Remove rings, belts, shoes and tight clothing before swelling occurs.
- Do not remove clothing that is stuck to the injury.
- Do not apply lotions, ointments or powders.
- Cover the burn loosely with a clean, dry cloth (e.g. handkerchief).

- Burns to the face or front of the torso may indicate burns to the airway which could lead to breathing difficulties.
SEEK MEDICAL ASSISTANCE.

SMOKE INHALATION

A person suffering from smoke inhalation may have breathing difficulties due to swelling or spasms of the air passage and may be confused or unconscious. CALL AN AMBULANCE (000).

- Turn the person on their back, arms above the head and drag them to safety and away from the smoke area.
- Keep yourself and the casualty low where there is less smoke.
- A person suffering from smoke inhalation may stop breathing. Check and if necessary perform Expired Air Resuscitation (EAR – you will learn this in a first-aid course, or refer to your *First Aid Quick Reference* from St John Ambulance).

EYES

Fires may result in smoke irritation or foreign bodies in the eyes.

- Discourage the person from rubbing their eyes.
- Flush the eye with water.

- Seek medical attention to remove foreign bodies if the above has not worked.

SHOCK

Shock can be a life-threatening condition, so if you suspect a person is suffering from shock, SEEK MEDICAL ATTENTION. A person suffering from shock may be vomiting or shaking, pale, sweating, confused or unconscious, have a rapid or weak pulse or abnormal breathing.

- Reassure the person.
- Moisten the lips but give no food or water.
- If unconscious turn the person on their side, monitor their breathing and circulation (pulse) and, if necessary, apply EAR.
- Raise their legs above the level of their heart.
- Continue to monitor breathing and pulse.
- Keep them warm.
- Treat any wounds.

BREAKS, SPRAINS AND BLEEDING

These injuries often occur during clean-up after a fire.

- Make the person comfortable.
- To stop bleeding, elevate the wound area, press the edges of the wound together and apply pressure with a clean pad or dressing.

- If a limb is broken, support the injured limb in the found position and splint the fracture – immobilise the joint above and below the fracture.
- If there is a sprain, apply a firm bandage, elevate the limb and apply cold compresses for 15 minutes every two hours for 24 hours.
- Reassure the person and treat them for shock if necessary.
- SEEK MEDICAL ATTENTION.

© St John Ambulance Australia
This information is not a substitute for first-aid training. St John recommends that everyone is trained in first-aid.

For more information about St John visit **www.stjohn.org.au** or call **1300 360 455**.

SEVEN

FREQUENTLY ASKED QUESTIONS

There is a lot of misinformation about bushfires. This chapter helps to separate fact from fiction and promote general understanding of bushfires.

Are you obliged to leave your home with the approach of a fire if told to do so by a member of the police force or an official from an emergency service?

This is a grey area of the law as there is variation from State to State regarding mandatory evacuation rules. However police and emergency services do have the power to order residents to evacuate if required. If this order is met with a refusal it could technically be a breach of the law but it is usually left to the resident to make the final decision. It is strongly recommended that a check be made with your local law enforcement agencies to determine your position in such a situation.

Is hazard-reduction burning a good idea?

This rather emotive question has generated a lot of debate for many years. Opponents of hazard-reduction burns are concerned about the risks to wildlife and their habitat, pollution and the possibility that controlled burns may get out of hand. However, the general consensus of expert opinion is that hazard reduction burns help minimise the occurrence of major bushfires. The theory is that burning off areas of bushland outside the fire season reduces the fuel load before the dangerous season, and subsequent fires will be less intense. Hazard-reduction burns are normally conducted by local fire brigades, who start fires in areas where the build-up of fuel is considered to be dangerous. Burns are carefully planned, often in consultation with the local Bureau of Meteorology office, to avoid periods of strong winds and low humidity. Paradoxically, the type of weather suitable for hazard-reduction burns is sometimes conducive to a build-up of smoke, and capital cities have sometimes been blanketed with smoke pollution following hazard-reduction burns in the suburbs. Hazard reduction does not always have to involve burning.

Raking up leaves and small sticks, clearing gutters around the house, mowing, clearing a firebreak (see page 23), ploughing or bulldozing are all examples of hazard reduction without burning.

Can bushfires produce rain?

When a big fire takes hold it generates a huge amount of energy, some of which creates powerful updraughts of air above the blaze. If sufficiently strong, these updraughts can actually produce a cloud – known as pyrocumulus – that rides above the fire. If this cloud grows tall enough it can even generate a shower of rain – a sort of natural fire extinguisher. Unfortunately, these clouds rarely produce enough water to make any real impression on the fire.

Can a fire jump a river?

Yes. Burning debris from a fire can be transported aloft and carried considerable distances by the prevailing winds to ignite fresh blazes, often on the other side of a waterway. In the 1967 Hobart bushfires, the blaze jumped the ocean to Bruny Island, a distance of approximately 6 km.

Can fires be seen from space?

Smoke from large bushfires is clearly visible from space vehicles. Bureau of Meteorology photographs taken from space above south-eastern Australia during the NSW fires of December 2019 show numerous smoke plumes blowing out to sea from inland sources close to the coast. Smoke was detected in New Zealand from these fires. Such photographs taken after bushfires also help to determine how much countryside has been burnt and to assess the general damage.

Boiled alive – fact or fiction?

Many people are sceptical of the notion that people can be boiled alive after plunging into a galvanised iron water tank to seek shelter from a bushfire. But unfortunately this is true. A tragic example took place during the catastrophic fires across Victoria on Friday 13 January 1939, when the tiny timber town of Matlock was engulfed by flames. One man tried to escape the blaze by jumping into a water tank that stood some 4 m above the ground, but was subsequently boiled alive as the flames swept through.

What are fire tornadoes?

As we saw in the discussion on pyrocumulus (page 69), large fires are capable of producing very strong updraughts of wind above the fire. In certain situations, possibly due to irregular terrain, changes in the prevailing winds or varying temperatures within the fire itself, these updraughts can begin to rotate. In extreme blazes, rotating columns of fire can achieve the strength of tornadoes and inflict terrible damage on the surroundings.

During the Canberra fires of 2003, fire tornadoes destroyed house roofs, twisted and snapped off trees and threw debris high in the air. It is believed that some of these fire tornadoes produced wind speeds of up to 300 kmph.

Can a cigarette butt really start a fire?

Research and experimentation has shown that a discarded still burning cigarette butt can definitely start a bushfire, although the weather and vegetation also play a big part. Some types of vegetation are far more flammable than others and, of course, during conditions of extreme fire danger undergrowth is more likely to ignite on contact with a cigarette butt. The situation is exacerbated along highways in bush areas, where careless motorists sometimes flick butts from their car window while travelling. If numerous butts have been discarded into dry vegetation on a hot, windy day with low humidity, the risks of a fire starting along the roadside are great.

The lesson is clear. DO NOT THROW CIGARETTE BUTTS FROM CAR WINDOWS.

In what other ways can human activity accidentally start fires?

Fires can be ignited by sparks produced when power lines swing into contact with each other, hot particles from rough-running engine exhausts, inappropriate burning-off operations, arson and the running of certain types of machinery, particularly on farms.

How frequent are bushfires?

The frequency of a bushfire impacting on a particular location, such as an individual property, is around once in every 20 years for south-eastern Australia but more frequent when a bigger area is considered.

The effect of climate change on bushfires is real and with rising temperatures the chance of more frequent and severe fires appears to be increasing.

Rising population, particularly in rural areas, also results in more fires because of human activity, including deliberate arson.

How fast do fires spread?

Numerous eyewitness reports and sensational media accounts in the past have reported fire fronts moving at tremendous speed, with people in cars unable to outpace the approaching fire front. However, in reality fires cannot travel at these sorts of speeds. Grass fires are certainly fast and measurements have shown that they can fly across the ground at about 25 kmph in hot, dry and windy conditions. This is equivalent to covering 100 m in about 14.4 seconds, which is a respectable sprint pace for a human, but for non-athletes such a pace could not be maintained for more than 20 seconds or so. In this case it would be virtually impossible to outrun the fire on foot, but entirely possible in a car. Forest fires are slower, with speeds of 15 kmph possible in severe situations. This represents 100 m in 24 seconds, which is only a moderately fast jog. However, severe fires can burn on several fronts, and spot fires can begin well ahead of the main front. This possibly accounts for the exaggerated accounts of fire front speed.

Are many fires deliberately lit?

Although the exact figures are not known, the deliberate lighting of bushfires is a significant problem. Indeed, it has been argued that the publicity surrounding the forecasting of extreme fire danger and imposition of total fire bans actually encourages arsonists.

This problem has been recognised at government level, and various strategies have been implemented accordingly. For example, an innovative program has been initiated by the Queensland Fire and Rescue Service called 'Fight Fire Fascination' (FFF). It targets the large number of children that have lit fires in the past.

The FFF program takes an educative rather than punitive approach. Trained firefighters personally visit families whose children have lit fires, to explain the dangers of their actions. The program has been highly successful in modifying the behaviour of such children.

Adult arsonists are more of a problem. They tend to be highly secretive in their actions. Ironically, some arsonists have been firefighters themselves, indicating the possibility of a mental illness related to a fascination with fire. This is in fact a recognised but difficult-to-treat psychological condition called 'pyromania'.

Every State imposes hefty penalties, including jail sentences, on those who deliberately light bushfires.

What is back burning?

Not to be confused with hazard-reduction burning, which is carried out before a bushfire begins, back burning is designed to slow the rate of progress of an aggressively advancing bushfire. This is done by lighting a fire ahead of the main blaze in an attempt to starve it of fuel. As the bushfire reaches the area already burned it usually moderates and reduces speed substantially. However, this is a potentially dangerous operation and should only be attempted through the specific advice and order of a firefighting agency.

How hot can bushfires get?

Temperatures near a fire vary considerably. Near the fire but not actually in the flames it can get as hot as 250°C. Inside the flames of an intense fire temperatures can exceed 1000°C and become hot enough to melt metals such as copper and aluminium. These variations in temperature can make the difference between vegetation being merely scorched or totally reduced to ashes.

An important feature of fires is their effect on soil temperature. Soil is a very effective insulator against fire. The surface temperature in a fire has been known to reach over 650°C, but a mere 22 cm below the surface, it has dropped to around 100°C.

The consequences of this are obvious. If you are caught in the open in a fire, covering yourself with soil, particularly over a damp blanket, can greatly increase your chance of survival as the flames pass across (see page 52).

Is it true that you should never walk on fallen tree trunks after a fire?

This is certainly the case. Even several days after a bushfire has been brought under control, tree trunks can continue smouldering. The upper side may appear only lightly scorched, offering an apparently safe foothold, but the middle and lower sections could have been burnt out. The log could disintegrate when you step on it and your foot may plunge through the top of the log into a bed of hot coals, resulting in severe burns.

Must a resident make water from his or her swimming pool available for helicopter firefighting crews?

The short answer is yes. During a fire emergency, water may be commandeered from a private dam or swimming pool for firefighting purposes. This may well take the form of a helicopter hovering above and dipping a bucket into the water supply before flying off to the fire and subsequently returning several times. If possible the fire authorities would consult with the property owner before this occurred but if, for example, the owner was away, this activity could commence without permission. In some States, a swimming pool owner can claim compensation for water lost in this way.

EIGHT

FIREFIGHTING EQUIPMENT

Useful tools and equipment for fighting fires, much of which you would already have in your shed or garage, are listed on pages 33–34. This section details more complex equipment, in particular the large-scale firefighting equipment used by bushfire brigades.

Firefighting Sprinkler Systems

In addition to using your garden sprinklers to help protect your home from fire, special firefighting sprinkler systems have saved many houses from being destroyed by bushfires. These usually consist of a series of pipes connected to an independent water supply such as a large tank, dam or swimming pool. Don't rely on mains water pressure to power the system, as this can fall considerably during a bushfire. Instead, use a portable petrol- or diesel-powered pump located in a protected position away from any possible fire hot spot. Don't rely on mains electricity either as the lines are often cut during a fire. Maintain the pump in good working order and test start it regularly to make sure it will be serviceable when required.

Metal pipes are ideal, but if plastic or rubber hoses are used they must be buried to avoid the radiant heat from the fire. However, sprinkler heads should be metal; plastic units will almost certainly melt when the fire approaches.

Site your system so that water spray can reach any areas where burning embers may lodge, such as under eaves, on verandahs, or in garden plots near the house. You can either install your own sprinkler system or have a professional install one to suit your budget.

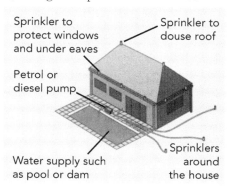

Sprinkler to protect windows and under eaves

Sprinkler to douse roof

Petrol or diesel pump

Water supply such as pool or dam

Sprinklers around the house

Road Tankers

Most bush fire brigades are equipped with at least one road going water tanker, which consists of a large tank mounted on a truck, with a mechanical pumping system that enables a stream of water to be sprayed on the fire through hoses.

These vehicles are often driven close to the fire frontline, and as such are frequently involved in highly dangerous situations. Modern tankers are usually equipped with a sprinkler system that surrounds them with water spray, protecting the vehicle and its occupants from at least some of the radiant heat of the fire. Nevertheless, firefighters have been killed in several tragedies due to so-called 'burnovers' in which their vehicle has been overtaken by flames.

When travelling to fire emergencies, tankers are normally equipped with sirens. On hearing the siren, motorists should pull over to give the tanker an unimpeded run.

Aircraft

In 2003 the National Aerial Firefighting Centre (NAFC) was formed to provide a coordinated national response to fight fires using aircraft – known as firebombing or aerial firefighting. This has revolutionised bushfire control for several reasons, including the fact that aircraft can reach areas of bushland inaccessible to ground crews, and then attack the centre of the blaze from above.

Water can be used, in addition to fire retardant chemicals that are highly effective in slowing down or even extinguishing large fires.

These aircraft are also very useful in identifying the location, extent and speed of movement of the fires, a process sometimes impossible from the ground.

Both fixed-wing aircraft and helicopters are used in this way.

FIXED-WING AIRCRAFT

Fixed-wing aircraft commonly used are the agricultural aeroplanes normally used in crop-dusting. These are capable of carrying 3000 L of water or fire retardant and flying at low altitudes to deliver their payloads.

One of the more exciting additions to the NAFC fleet is the B737 Large Air Tanker, a twin-engine jet aircraft that can lift an astonishing 15,000 litres of water, fire retardant or foam to target the fires. The sheer speed and capacity of this aircraft make it a powerful firefighting force.

Perhaps surprisingly it can fly at quite low altitude and is manoeuvrable enough to travel across rugged terrain.

HELICOPTERS

The use of helicopters for firefighting has become one of the major success stories of modern firefighting. They carry fixed tanks or buckets attached to a cable and are capable of replenishing their water supply in flight by dipping the bucket into the sea, a lake or dam, or even a swimming pool in a residential area. This capability, as well as their ability to hover, means they can deliver a constant stream of water into the heart of a fire.

One of the best known of the helicopter fleet is the Erikson Aircrane, a machine that can hover-fill and deliver over 7000 L of water or fire retardant over the blaze.

Fire-bombing aircraft always need to be supported by firefighting ground crews who battle the small fires not extinguished by the aircraft. However, aerial fire bombing has been a tremendous boon to fire safety over much of Australia.

NINE

DESIGNING A FIRE-RESISTANT HOME

If you are contemplating moving to the country and building your dream home in 'the bush', plan for 'fire-smart' design right from the beginning of your project.

❏ Prevent intrusion of wind-borne burning material by using close-fitting windows and doors. Use non-flammable aluminium frames in preference to wooden ones.

❏ Avoid or minimise firetraps like decorative wooden trellises and latticework and wooden verandahs and balconies.

❏ Build the house on a concrete slab to reduce the chance of burning material rolling under the house.

❏ On a sloping block set the house into the slope rather than building it jutting out over the ground, exposing the underside of the floor to flames moving up the slope.

❏ Use a simple roof design to minimise hidden angles and traps where dried vegetation can accumulate and become a fire hazard.

❏ Avoid skylights, which are a weak point in any roof. Falling branches can punch through a skylight more readily than through normal roof surfaces.

❏ Provide accessible ceiling 'manholes' to allow easy entry to the inside of the roof to extinguish small blazes during a bushfire.

❏ Steel roofing is probably the safest, but remember that 'rippled' galvanised iron exposes the roof space below to possible ember intrusion.

❏ Traditional wooden shingles or thatching, which have enjoyed a revived popularity in recent times, are entirely unsuitable for a home in the Australian bush.

❏ Avoid flammable bituminous membranes or roof sealing compounds.

❏ Ensure that the roofing material is well anchored to the underlying structure to withstand the strong winds that often accompany fires.

❏ Guttering is the most problematic area to fire proof on a roof. In a bush environment with surrounding eucalypt trees, a constant 'shower' of leaves will quickly fill gutters. The roof itself will also be coated with leaves and twigs, which will wash into the gutters when it rains, often clogging the down pipes. In thick bushland settings gutters will need to be cleared weekly.

To avoid these problems, use a 'leafless' guttering that is covered with mesh to keep twigs and leaves out. Although more expensive, this type of guttering is a good investment, particularly in the reduction or even elimination of the unpleasant, time-consuming and dangerous task of gutter clearing.

Some homes feature so-called 'gutterless' construction. The water simply flows off the roof directly to the ground. This solves the problem of blocked gutters, but to avoid water damage to the house foundations, you need to construct special surface drains around the perimeter of the building. Council permission may also be required to approve this type of construction.

❏ If the floor of the house has to be elevated, ensure that the supports are non-flammable. Ideally the space between the ground and the floor should be bricked in.

SMOKE ALARMS

Contrary to popular opinion, smoke alarms can be useful in bushfire situations, particularly overnight when people are sleeping.

Although bushfires normally slow down at night as wind and temperatures drop, there are exceptions. For example, strong winds may be whipped up ahead of an approaching cold front, causing fires to flare and spread with renewed vigour even at night.

In such circumstances a smoke alarm can alert sleeping occupants that smoke is increasing in the home, either as a result of a fire approaching outside, or because a fire has begun inside as a result of the intrusion of flying embers.

Smoke alarms should be of a reputable brand and be sited and installed according to the manufacturer's instructions. They should also be tested regularly to ensure that the power supply, whether mains or battery, is operational and that the unit is fully functional.

TEN

THE AUSTRALIAN BUSHFIRES OF 2019 – 2020

Unprecedented Fires

Bushfires over Australia burned through massive areas of the mainland and smaller parts of Tasmania from October 2019 across to the summer months of 2020. In terms of longevity and extent the fires were unprecedented in Australia's recorded bushfire history.

Over six million hectares of land were burned and up until early January at least 25 people had lost their lives.

In December 2019, NSW Rural Fire Services Commissioner Shane Fitzsimmons said it was 'absolutely' the worst bushfire season on record.

Longevity

The extraordinary longevity of the fires was a standout with major blazes continuing to flare over several weeks, in contrast to the 'short sharp' fire disasters of Black Friday (1939), Ash Wednesday (1983) and Black Saturday (2009). These latter fires were short-term in comparison, with the worst of the blazes lasting around 48 hours, whereas the 2019/20 fires were spread across an extended period of three to four months in some areas.

Smoke impact

The impact of the fires was also pronounced over Sydney, Melbourne and Canberra where thick smoke settled for extended periods, producing poor air quality and health issues, particularly for those with existing respiratory problems such as asthma. This meant that the social impact of the fires was massive, even for those not directly impacted.

And the smoke had an international effect as well. Massive palls rolled across the Tasman Sea with skies across New Zealand turning yellow and glaciers tinted brown from the smoke and dust that had travelled some 2000 kilometres.

Extent of the fires

As well as the longevity of the fires, the geographic extent of the affected areas was also unprecedented. Fires stretched from southern Queensland, southwards into NSW and then the Gippsland area of Victoria. A large fire swathe cut through the Adelaide Hills, an area north of Perth, and even parts of the east coast of Tasmania.

Existing fires continued to spread and enlarge from early October 2019, with record low rainfall and high temperatures exacerbating the situation. Fires that were dormant became reactivated each time there was a spike in wind and temperature and they continued to grow in size. The sheer extent of the blazes meant that it was never going to be possible to extinguish them using human intervention.

Several of the fires devastated towns across eastern Victoria and the south coast of New South Wales including Batemans Bay, Balmoral, Lake Conjola, Mogo, Cobargo, Mallacoota and across large swathes of the East Gippsland area. These were all tragic events producing loss of life and widespread property damage, including hundreds of houses, and forced thousands of people to relocate and seek shelter in other areas. In South Australia, a large part of Kangaroo Island was burned out with a fast moving blaze that tragically took the lives of two men who were caught in their car.

The Gospers Mountain Fire

Some of the individual blazes within this big picture were also remarkable. The Gospers Mountain fire, near the New South Wales Central Coast, started in late October – likely through a lightning strike – and continued to burn for weeks after, growing on a daily basis. It soon assumed proportions that proved too large for fire fighters to extinguish and became a 'fire reservoir' that burst across the surrounding countryside with every surge of wind and temperature. The only real control possible was around the fringes of the fire using aerial bombing.

Experts believed that the blaze was the largest single ignition point forest fire in Australia and was larger than any single Californian or Mediterranean forest fire.

Rainforest Fires

It was not only the highly flammable eucalyptus forests that were burned. Areas of sub-tropical rainforest, not normally susceptible to bushfires because of their perpetually 'damp' growth pattern, also experienced extensive blazes.

This included the unique and World Heritage-listed 'Gondwana' rainforests of northeast NSW and Southeast Queensland, considered to be the last living links with the ancient continent of Gondwanaland. This was the southern hemisphere 'supercontinent', that broke apart under the influence of continental drift some 180 million years ago. The fires also threatened the ancient Wollemi Pine, whose survival was only discovered in 1994 when a few stands were found in a remote and rugged area around

150 kilometres to the northwest of Sydney. This area became part of the Gospers Mountain fire.

Some frightening stories

Many extraordinary events took place during the fires with numerous tales of tragedy, property damage and dramatic escapes that produced headline news across the country.

The world renowned Mogo Zoo, located on the south coast of New South Wales, contains a large variety of exotic animals, including monkeys, pandas, giraffes, zebras, lions, tigers and orangutans. On the morning of 31 December 2019 an evacuation order was issued for the zoo, but the staff elected to stay and defend, as they had in place a detailed and well-prepared fire plan. They also had good coverage from water pumps, including well-equipped vehicles and the area all across the property was thoroughly watered down.

Many of the smaller animals were evacuated to safe locations nearby and the large and dangerous animals such as the big cats were placed in their night dens, and as far as possible kept calm.

Despite the ferocity of the fire, no animals were lost, providing a good illustration of a successful fire defence, made possible because of careful planning and the availability of water and proper equipment.

On the same day a fire crew travelling to a job in their truck near Nowra, on the NSW south coast, were caught as flames surged across the road and swept over their vehicle. One of the firemen recorded the incident from inside, showing the red flames and streams of glowing embers blasting over the truck against a near black sky above. This is known as a 'burnover' and in past examples fatalities have followed.

However in this case the truck kept going despite being partially melted on one side and the crew were able to exit the flames and reach safe ground.

The Wildlife Situation

As well as the tragic human death toll one of the more significant impacts of the fires concerned the effects on wildlife – in particular koalas – that attracted much of the associated publicity. It was estimated that up to 30% of the koala population on the New South Wales mid-north-coast may have perished in the fires. However significant mortality was also experienced across many other species, such as flying foxes, wombats, and several species of birds.

The B737 Large Air Tanker

One of the most spectacular and effective fire fighting devices used during the event was the B737 Large Air Tanker (LAT), a twin-engine jet aircraft capable of carrying 15,000 litres of fire retardant. The B737 is a converted Boeing 737 airliner whose 72 passenger seats have been removed to allow it to carry the fire retardant at altitudes as low as 50 metres.

The retardant is a liquid containing phosphate fertiliser that reduces the speed and temperature of the blaze, and if dropped accurately, can knock out the fire below, at least temporarily. It is coloured pink, so that the pilot can see what areas have been hit and judge his subsequent 'runs' accordingly. It is also a useful marker for ground crews following up after the aircraft has departed.

The B737 was particularly useful in halting blazes that were approaching housing, with the low altitude retardant dumps providing spectacular television imagery across all the national news services.

Management of the Fires

Also rolled out publically for the first time was the internet-based 'Fires Near Me' software package that proved to be a highly popular and heavily used resource. Used by the NSW Rural Fire Service, similar information packages were also utilised in other States.

Regularly and frequently updated these information portals showed the location and intensity of all fires burning, and included information on alert levels, council areas affected, status, and type and size of the blaze. This information became a valuable public resource, and was widely used as a basis for general decision-making.

The fire management itself was very well conducted with timely evacuations launched from many areas well before the fires hit. The public generally responded well to the wishes of the authorities and this was at least partly the result of the public education campaigns previously conducted by the various fire commands.

The Social Impacts

The social impacts of the fires were massive, assisted by the high visibility of the event – in particular the frequent smoke palls across our capital cities. Sydney, Melbourne and Canberra were heavily affected, meaning that something like 43% of the population of Australia were exposed to smoke in some way during the time of the fires

– that is more than 10 million based on 2018 population figures.

Saturation media coverage kept public awareness high for an extended period and helped generate considerable debate about the connections between climate change and bushfires. This debate had a considerable polarising effect across the country with a great deal of direct attention moving away from the fires towards discussions and debates about climate change. Bushfires often become political events and this was certainly the case here.

There was also lengthy discussion about using the military in some role in the fire-fighting process, either as personnel on the ground or involved in the logistical chain as providers of transport, rations, field kitchens and general supplies. Early in January there was increasing involvement of the military, in particular the Army Reserve and the Navy.

The economic impact of the fires was immense – from several different standpoints. The summer tourist industry, that is the backbone of many of the small coastal townships in both New South Wales and Victoria, was devastated with cancellations. The insurance bill ran up over $600 million, with national premiums affected as a result. The actual damage bill was significantly higher as many property owners were under-insured – or carried no insurance at all.

References

Bushfire Weather, Bureau of Meteorology brochure, Melbourne, 2004

CSIRO web site: www.cmit.csiro.au/innovation/2003–10/bushfires.cfm

Drought, Dust and Deluge, Bureau of Meteorology, Melbourne, 2004

NSW Rural Fire Service www.bushfire.nsw.gov.au

Preparing for the Unexpected, Emergency Management Australia booklet, Commonwealth of Australia, 2003

Webster, J. 2000 *The Complete Bushfire Safety Book*, Random House, Sydney

Whitaker, R. & Calls, K. 2001, *The Australian Weather Book*, Reed New Holland, Sydney

Attributions

Photograph on page 70 courtesy of earthobservatory.nasa.gov.

Map on page 8 redrawn by Andrew Davies from a Bureau of Meteorology map.

INDEX